☛ Three Creepy Plays ☚

"The Witch Makes Five"

"Forty Whacks"

and

"Hockey Masks in Hueytown"

by
John Glass

john@studentplays.org

<u>Copyright information. Please read!</u>

☞ About Student Plays ☜

Student Plays consists of **John Glass, Jackie Jernigan,** and **Dominic Torres.** We are a group of playwrights and directors that have written scripts for elementary school through college. We are proud of the variety of ages that our scripts serve.

Student Plays has "creepy" plays, and we also have Latino-themed plays. These are scripts that focus on Latino youths and the Latino experience. Any school can perform a Latino-themed play: it just requires a general introduction and basic exposure to the Spanish language, something that most schools and students already have.

To contact *Student Plays* or to communicate with one of the playwrights, simply email us at john@studentplays.org.

The Witch Makes Five

-

A one-act play

by
John Glass

☞   ☞

Characters of the Play

JOYCE: High School Student. Distraught. Agitated.

ROD: High School Student. Nervous.

STACIE: High School Student. Nervous.

WORKER 1   Either gender. Small role at the play's end.

WORKER 2   Either gender. Small role at the play's end.

The setting is a patient's room in a mental treatment center for the youth. JOYCE is a patient and is being visited by ROD and STACIE. She is wearing a hospital/facility gown or shirt. There are a few chairs, a small table with a telephone, and if possible, a bed or cot. Everyone is shaken and somewhat uncomfortable.

The time is the present, October, and there are several Halloween decorations hanging about. A witch face should be one of the decorations, prominently displayed.

This ten-minute play is best suited for middle school, high school, or even college. The few allusions to "high school student" and so forth can easily be altered, if necessary.

At RISE: ROD and JOYCE are seated, in the middle of discussion.

ROD: Well, I'll tell you one thing.

JOYCE: What?

ROD: I'm never going camping again.

JOYCE: Man. No kidding!

ROD: And I'm also never going to go looking for *anything* in the middle of the woods. Stupid *StoneHouse* . . .

JOYCE: Well, let's be honest: something tells me the StoneHouse found *us*.

ROD: Tell me about it *(Beat.)* But you know what was really cool?

JOYCE: What?

ROD: Those wicked-looking pine trees! In the moonlight!

JOYCE: Don't start with the pine trees!

ROD: Seriously, Joyce. I wasn't going to mention it. But the way those needles silhouetted against the moon! Wow . . .

JOYCE: You are such a writer.

ROD: Come on, it was beautiful. We've got to find something positive out of all this. Right?

JOYCE: Um, I guess.

ROD: It was exotic.

JOYCE: Look. I don't want us to keep ignoring this. You know what we saw. Don't you?

ROD: Well . . . *(Uncomfortably)* I know what I *think* I saw.

JOYCE: You mean, you *know* what you saw.

ROD: Hmmph.

JOYCE: Come on, Stacie saw her too. Let's not pretend. Okay?

ROD: *(Quietly.)* Yeah. I know.

JOYCE: We all saw her. *(Beat. She is very distraught.)* But . . . Rod?

ROD: What?

JOYCE: You know what I absolutely *can't* pretend about that camping trip? I know we agreed to drop this for now. But Rod . . . there were four of us out there. *Four* of us!

ROD: Look, Joyce—

(Enter STACIE, carrying a small bottle/can of juice. She sets it down.)

JOYCE: *(Grabbing him by the arm.)* I know, I know. You guys think I lost it out in those woods. Both of you do!

ROD: I didn't say that!

STACIE: *(Groaning, at hearing the discussion)* Ughh!

JOYCE: But it was you, me, Stacie . . . and *Scottie*! Scottie was the one that organized the whole camping trip!

ROD: Joyce—

JOYCE: You guys have known him since that film class our freshman year! And I've known him for almost that long!

STACIE: Joyce? We know that you—

JOYCE: Oh, don't start, Stacie. I know what you're thinking! You've already said that I belong in here. That this place might be good for me for a little while.

STACIE: You know that I didn't mean it like that! Come on!

JOYCE: Whatever.

ROD: Joyce, it's just that we've already told you. We don't know a *Scottie!* We never have! It was you, Stacie and me! Three college idiots in the middle of the woods!

STACIE: Searching for something we never should have been looking for.

ROD: *(Slowly.)* Something . . *happened* out there, Joyce. Something really bizarre.

STACIE: Right.

ROD: Something that affected you.

JOYCE: Stacie, you believe that we saw something. Don't you?

(Pause. STACIE sits, and speaks slowly.)

STACIE: Oh, yeah. Absolutely. I told you that I did. That face . . . I can't get it out of my brain.

JOYCE: Okay. So if you remember that, don't you remember how Scottie walked right up to that window? Holding that flashlight?? Scottie was the first one to see her!!

STACIE: Joyce, that didn't happen! *Rod* was holding the flashlight! There *was* no Scottie! There were only *three* of us out there, Joyce.

JOYCE: There were FOUR OF US!! Us three, and *Scottie*!!
>   *(Pause.)*
And that . . that *witch*. The witch makes five.
>   *(Off their look.)*
Don't look at me like that!

ROD: Joyce, take your medication.

JOYCE: Ughhh.

STACIE: Yeah, here's the juice.

JOYCE: I don't have the pills yet. The nurse should be bringing them in a minute.

ROD: Okay. Well . . . relax. You're okay.

JOYCE: And anyway, I need water. The doctor said not to take medication with juice.

ROD: I'll go get some water.

STACIE: Sorry, I'll get it.

ROD: No, it's fine, I got it. There's a fountain down the hall.

JOYCE: There are cups in the nurse's office.

ROD: Be right back.

JOYCE: Thanks, Rod.

(Pause as he exits. JOYCE attempts to collect herself.)

JOYCE: I'm sorry, Stacie.

STACIE: It's okay. Just try and stay calm.

JOYCE: I know. I know.

STACIE: You'll be out of this place in no time.

JOYCE: I hope . . . *(Pause. She sighs, looks around the room.)* Damn. Do they have to have these stupid Halloween decorations in here?

STACIE: Well, it *is* October.

JOYCE: I know . . . but sheesh. I'm already freaked out as it is.
(Beat. Still distraught.)
I apologize, Stacie. I'm just a wreck.

STACIE: It's fine.

JOYCE: No, I'm really a wreck. I'm eighteen years old and I had a nervous breakdown. What teenager does that?
(Beat.)
And my parents, wow, they're all upset. I had to practically beg them to leave this afternoon, to get away for a few hours. To go grab some dinner.

STACIE: I talked to your teachers. They all know you'll be out of school for a bit.

JOYCE: Aggh! My classes!

STACIE: It's fine. They understood. You'll be out of here soon. Your teachers don't know *exactly* what you're going through but they know that it's serious.

JOYCE: Well, what we went through *was* serious.

STACIE: Gosh . . . don't remind me. It's . . . the *explaining* part that's eventually going to be tough. For *all* of us.

(Pause as they reflect.)

JOYCE: I can still see her. Her face. Uggh. Those wrinkled, bony hands, holding that candle. So vicious and dark.

STACIE: *(Slowly.)* Nobody knows, Joyce. Nobody.

JOYCE: What??

STACIE: I didn't tell anyone. About her.

JOYCE: Are you serious? No one??

STACIE: I mean . . . how can I? My parents don't know, or anyone else. I don't know if I'll ever tell a single person. *(Slowly.)* I just don't want to . . .

JOYCE: . . end up in here like I did?

STACIE: No. I didn't say that.

JOYCE: Well. You don't *have* to. It's all over your face.

STACIE: I'm sorry. I–

JOYCE: *(Holding a hand up.)* Don't. It's fine. I understand.

>*(Pause. They gather themselves, uncomfortably.)*

STACIE: Okay. Well. Yeah. Stupid StoneHouse.

JOYCE: I know . . .

STACIE: Stupid witch.

>*(Beat. JOYCE attempts to lighten things up.)*

JOYCE: And Rod! Ha! Rod screamed like a little girl!

>*(Pause as she laughs. STACIE stares at her in confusion.)*

STACIE: Who . . ?

JOYCE: *Rod,* Stacie. Our friend.

STACIE: Who the heck are you talking about?

JOYCE: ROD!! *(She jumps up and paces in anger.)* Oh, what is HAPPENING here?? First Scottie, and now Rod??

STACIE: Joyce—

JOYCE: He's our *friend*, Stacie! He's down the hall, getting water for my medication!

STACIE: Who are you talking about?? Nobody came to visit you but me!!

JOYCE: You came with Rod!! Our goofball writer friend!! *Rod,* Stacie! We went camping with him this weekend!!

STACIE: Joyce, I don't know a *Rod!* Or a *Scottie*! You and me went camping, and you and me *only*.

JOYCE: No!

STACIE: Joyce, get a grip of yourself!

JOYCE: I've *got* a grip of myself! It's everybody else I'm worried about!! *(Tears down the witch decoration.)* I should have taken that down a long time ago!

STACIE: Look, I'm going to call one of the nurses. *(Moves to pick up the phone.)*

JOYCE: *(Calling down the hallway.)* ROD?? Rod, get in here! Rod!!

STACIE: *(On phone)* Hello . .? Hello! I need help in Room 8!

JOYCE: ROD!

(She exits, calling his name.)

STACIE: Joyce, come back! *(Back on phone.)* Hello? Is anyone there?? Hello??
(Pause.)
Oh, yes, I am in room 8, and I really need your help! The patient here just ran out!
(Pause.)
What?? What do you mean, *there's no patient in this room*?? Joyce Carol is in this room! Room 8!
(Pause. She repeats herself.)
Her name is Joyce Carol! I'm here visiting her! Hello? Did you hear me?? HELLO??
(Slams the phone down. She turns to the hall way, and begins to exit.)
JOYCE?? JOYCE!!

(She runs out, calling her name. Long pause. Enter two workers from the other side of the stage. They are carrying a broom, cleaning materials, and a clipboard with papers.)

WORKER ONE: You brought the dustpan, didn't you?

WORKER TWO: Yep. Right here.

WORKER ONE: Okay. Nobody's been in here for a few days so it's probably a little dusty.

WORKER TWO: Can't believe how quiet it's been all day.

WORKER ONE: I know. It's like a ghost town.

WORKER TWO: I wish it were always this quiet.
(Pause as they work.)
How many do we have left to clean?

WORKER ONE: Two more. But they want this room ready by the morning, for a new patient.

WORKER TWO: Yeah.

WORKER ONE: *(Picking up the witch decoration.)*
Looks like one of the decorations fell off the wall.

WORKER TWO: Ugghh. I've never liked witches.

WORKER ONE: Ha. I've always liked them. This needs to go back on the wall.

WORKER TWO: Mmmm. If you say so . . .

(They continue working in silence. Lights fade. End of play.)

Forty Whacks

A one-act play

by
John Glass

☞

☞

Characters

MAX   Twenties or thirties. Kind. Deferring.

DIANA   Late twenties, early thirties. Aggressive.
                 Ambitious.

JACK   Only Jack's *voice* is heard, in a conversation
                 with Diana via speaker phone. It is a very
                 small part, at the beginning of Scene Three.
                 (This role could be doubled with the LIZZIE
                 role.)

LIZZIE BORDEN   The character herself. Twenties or
                    thirties. The role is extremely
                    minimal and has no dialogue.

The time is the present, and the setting is the Lizzie Borden
Bed and Breakfast, in Fall River, Massachusetts. It is
October. The entire play takes place in the front room of the
hotel, an old room with the décor from the 1890s. There is
a hotel desk, with a computer, telephone, clipboard and
various papers. A rack of keys is hanging on the wall
behind the desk. A portrait of Lizzie Borden is hanging.

If possible, there is also a sofa and a few easy chairs, and other usual furnishings.

The appearance by Lizzie at the very end of all three scenes is extremely simple and brief. During these brief scenes, if possible, a single light will shine on Diana, accompanied by a long note of music, something deep and mysterious; Lizzie Borden will then enter far stage right or stage left, and observe Diana from afar. She is holding a candle or a lantern.

SCENE ONE

Before the lights go up, the following audio is heard:

On August 4, 1892, the parents of Lizzie Borden were brutally hatcheted to death in their home in Fall Spring, Massachusetts. The evidence gradually pointed to Lizzie as a suspect, and she eventually was forced to stand trial for the murders. The trial attracted national attention, and even generated worldwide interest. However, on the 20th of June, 1893, in a courtroom in New Bedford, Massachusetts, Lizzie was found not guilty. Nonetheless, the legend of Lizzie Borden has become part of Americana, and has been established as one of the most macabre tales of our national heritage.

It is early Friday afternoon, and MAX and Diana are behind the desk, talking. As they talk they are working. Throughout this scene DIANA looks at and points to the large wall behind the desk.

DIANA: Think about it, Max. We could even have News 8 out here! The biggest excavation in Massachusetts history!

MAX: Excavation?

DIANA: Excavation. Wall tear-down. Whatever.

MAX: Sheesh.

(Pause.)

DIANA: Listen. I know Dad was always against things like this.

MAX: *And* Mom.

DIANA: Okay, Mom too. Maybe. But just think of what it could do for business! 'And here we are, folks, the hidden bottle of prussic acid! Still intact with the little skull and crossbones label on the back!'

MAX: Come off it! The Bordens were killed with an axe.

DIANA: But what *if* Lizzie first tried to poison them with the acid? You know that her parents were sick!

MAX: They were sick because they ate five-day-old mutton broth!

DIANA: That was never proved!

MAX: Ohhhh! Would you stop?
   (Beat.)
Damn, Diana . . . how many of those books *did* you read?

DIANA: I don't know. Come on. I never hung out here like you used to. I had to educate myself somehow.

MAX: So, how many?

DIANA: Uh. Four?

MAX: What?? Four books?

DIANA: Yes. And Max . . .? There's so many new theories out there. So much new research. After all these years, we could finally see a re-opening of the case! "We are here, folks, live with Diana and Max—the new owners of the Borden Hotel!"
> *(Off his face. Beat.)*
Okay, sorry, *Max and Diana*. Not *Diana and Max*. But look: it could be HUGE!

MAX: Stop.

DIANA: The prussic acid is that forgotten piece of evidence. I'd like to sort of capitalize on it.

MAX: Would you let it go, please?

DIANA: We could even put it on Twitter!

MAX: We are *not* putting this place on Twitter. It's bad enough that all those silly travel reporters are constantly out here.

DIANA: Okay. True. But we—

MAX: Did you have room 4 cleaned?

DIANA: I did, yes. Took care of it myself.

MAX: Okay. What about the toilet in room five?

DIANA: Uh, yeah. Ugghh. Done.

MAX: Okay.

> *(Pause. She collects herself. She slowly begins to experience a headache here, which gradually worsens.)*

DIANA: I just see so much potential here. The prussic acid theory could really give a jolt to our business. I'd like to try and make something out of it.

MAX: What about the paint job? You got your way on that, you know. And that's not going to be cheap!

DIANA: But look at how fresh the place is going to look!

MAX: *And* that TV commercial . . .

DIANA: Well . . .

MAX: Don't forget about the hotel discount thing you insisted on. I'm still not sure about *that* idea.

DIANA: *(Rubbing her head.)* I checked the books. Mom and Dad hadn't raised their prices in over eight years. You know how inflation works.

MAX: You really need to see a doctor about that.

DIANA: I am. I'm going on Monday.
>   *(Pause. She is in pain.)*
Oh, Max. You have no idea. The intensity . . . ohhh . . .

MAX: Do you need anything?

DIANA: No. No, it's fine. I've already taken aspirin.

MAX: Sure don't look like it.
>   *(Beat.)*
Look. I admit. You sort of know what you're doing. You've had your own business before.

DIANA: Yeah. Look how that turned out.

MAX: It doesn't matter. You were successful. You did well. You were just—just *unlucky.*

DIANA: Well . . . yeah.

MAX: I just want to make sure we're making wise decisions here, Diana. I know that it's almost Halloween, and business is good. But . . . I *need* this job. I need this income.

DIANA: I understand. We both do.

MAX: And I'd like to continue the decency that Mom and Dad maintained for so long. But . . . well, we had an agreement. Right?

DIANA: Yeah. I know.

MAX: So . . .?

DIANA: I know. If it really makes you uncomfortable, then I'll drop the whole idea.

MAX: Thank you. That *was* what we agreed on, right?

DIANA: Yes. Sorry for pushing.

MAX: Well. I just want to make sure we understand each other.

DIANA: We do.

    (Pause. MAX begins working on the computer.)

MAX: Okay. So let's see . . . Judy is here on Wednesday. Then you have the young guy coming in, right? The part-timer?

DIANA: Yes. William. I think his name is William. He's going to help Joanna in the gift shop too.
    (Beat. She notices a box on the floor.)
What's this box?

MAX: It was in the attic. Papers, old letters. It also has tax receipts that we need to look over. And some important coding and licensing stuff.

DIANA: Oh. Yeah. Good thinking.

MAX: There's a lot of other old papers in there I need to go through.

DIANA: Are you still heading up to Boston?

MAX: This afternoon.

DIANA: Getting the rest of your stuff?

MAX: Yep. Might go to the Cape with Jimmy and his wife. And some people are throwing me a good-bye party from the post office Saturday night. Ha – two months later.

DIANA: Enjoy yourself. I'll have everything covered here.

MAX: Cool.

DIANA: Max . . . ?

MAX: Yes?

> *(Pause. She looks directly at the wall. MAX remains busy, working.)*

DIANA: Aren't you at all curious? As to what might be inside that wall?

MAX: What I think . . . . is that Mom and Dad asked themselves that same question for the thirty years they were here. But you know what they would want us to do. Or *not* to do. If there really is a bottle of prussic acid stashed in there . . . then . . . well, I just don't know. Taking that out of the wall would be a complete spectacle. And Mom would never want us to do that. She's the reason it never happened.

DIANA: Mom developed more of an entrepreneurial spirit than you think.

MAX: Diana, how do you know? You weren't around her for almost five years!

DIANA: I talked to Mom off and on. We weren't exactly estranged.

MAX: I just think that a wall tear-down would be chaotic. We've already got so much going on here. I mean, what about that TV commercial? What station is that going to be on? The Chill Channel?

DIANA: Yes.

MAX: Lord. And the website! Do you *really* think it needs updating?

DIANA: Let me get back to you on that. This web guy told me he might be able to do it in exchange for a yearly pass for his grandparents. They apparently love this place.
> *(Beat.)*

Max, you have to admit. Wall tear-down or not, we can make this place into a *fine* business. Not just a *business.* Creepy things have become hip all of a sudden. Mom and Dad fell into a business rut, and I'd like to change that! Attendance is up—

MAX: It's Halloween. Attendance is always up. *(He looks at his paperwork, begins to exit.)*

DIANA: Well, isn't that a good thing?

MAX: Yes.

DIANA: Hell, it should be Halloween year-round!

MAX: Around here it is. And I don't think there's a person better suited for this job than you.

DIANA: Of course there isn't! And look: we can't deprive Lizzie of her time to shine!

MAX: Lord . . .

DIANA: Halloween weekend's going to be packed, right? We should create a sound system throughout the whole hotel! Rattle some chains in the middle of the night! Maybe a witch cackle!

MAX: We aren't doing that.

DIANA: Just an idea, just an idea.

MAX: Well, your ideas scare me. Alright, I've got to do the laundry. Answer the phone, will you?

DIANA: Of course.

(He exits. Diana moves to the wall area. Stage becomes dark except one single light on her. A deep chord or note accompanies this quick mini-scene. As she puts her hands to her temples, experiencing more pain, she produces a tape measure, and takes several measurements of the wall.)

*(**LIZZIE** slowly enters stage left, and silently watches her. She does not exit. The light and the music gradually fade, end of scene.)*

SCENE TWO

Monday morning, a few days later. As the lights go up,
MAX is talking on the phone.

MAX: Wow. You should be one of our platinum members
or something.
(Laughs.)
I mean, thirteen consecutive years. Wow. Well, thanks for
the business. Yes, Joanna is still here, out in the gift shop. I
left the post office, and Diana moved back after being out
in Tulsa for five years. Yeah. I sure didn't think we'd ever
wind up owning the place. But here we are.
(Pause. Enter DIANA, just waking up, very groggy.)
Okay. You are all set. Party of four, two rooms. Around
three p.m., October 25th. Great, thank you! Bye.
(Hangs up. Begins working on the computer.)
Wow. Two old couples that live in Maine, and they still
drive down here every year.

DIANA: Oh.

MAX: What's going on?

DIANA: Nothing. Trying to wake up. You're in here early.
(She gets a cup of coffee, gradually wakes up.)

MAX : Diana, it's nine o' clock.

DIANA: Oh. Shoot, so it is. Wow. Uh, how was the Cape?

MAX: We didn't make it out there. Just stayed in Boston the whole time.

DIANA: Oh.

MAX: We went to a Sox playoff game, and I got the rest of my stuff. It was clammy. That's one thing I bet you didn't miss about New England when you were away.

DIANA: Clammy weather beats tornados anytime.

MAX: Well. Yeah, I guess it does.

DIANA: Did you see the hallway? The new paint?

MAX: Yes. Looks okay, I guess. That's probably not the best for your migraines, though, you know. Paint fumes in the house.

DIANA: Oh. I actually hadn't thought about that.

MAX: Are you still having them?

DIANA: Not as bad. But yes. The doctor gave me pills but they've done nothing.
(Beat.)
But hey: here's the good news! Look at the reservation book.

MAX: I'm looking right at it. How on Earth are we doing all this business?

DIANA: Isn't it great? Reservations for December! I looked back at the old books, and I could never find any reservations made here during the week of Christmas.

MAX: Uh-huh. I wonder why.

DIANA: What are you saying?

MAX: Nothing, nothing.
(Sees a paper on desk. Beat.)
Oh. Are those students still coming out here to film their little documentary?

DIANA: Yep. This weekend, I believe.

MAX: Hmmph. They're just going to be *outside*, right? Getting footage of the house and neighborhood?

DIANA: Yeah, that's all. They're just college students. It's just some small project for their film class.

MAX: Hmmph.

DIANA: Don't start all that. That thing could be on TV one day. Those kinds of things are good for us. TV brings exposure, and more exposure means more business.

MAX: Well. True. But it's not . . . it's not always about the money, Diana. That's all.

DIANA: But at some point it has to be.

(The telephone rings. DIANA answers as MAX works at computer.)

DIANA: Good morning, the Borden House.
(Pause.)
We are out on Route 13, just past the Oyster Club. Yes. Exactly. About a mile past the Oyster Club. Okay, you're welcome.
(Hangs up. Pause as she looks at paperwork.)
So how many checkouts do we have?

MAX: Uh, four. Judy comes in at eleven, and William will be here at twelve. We can put them on the checkouts when they arrive.

DIANA: Okay.

(Beat. MAX notices something on the computer.)

MAX: Um. Wow. You let the web guy put those old pictures up already? Of the Bordens?

DIANA: Oh. Yes. We did talk about that, didn't we?

MAX: We talked about it. But that's about it.

DIANA: I'm sorry. I forgot if you were okay with that or not. I just went ahead and told him to do it.

MAX: I noticed. I'm looking right at it.

DIANA: You don't like it? Honestly, I think it helps bring in more customers.

MAX: It just seems a little macabre.

DIANA: Max, the whole house is macabre! That's what we're all about!

MAX: But showing bloody photographs . . . as a way of advertising?

DIANA: It helps people visualize what happened here. Come on, it's advertising! People need to see what we're all about. They can't just rely on . . . *(Sarcastically)* . . 'when she saw what she had done, she gave her father forty-one.'

(Pause. MAX puts his head down, stressed.)

DIANA: All right . . . look, how about this? I'll take down the picture of the mother's body. You know, the really bloody one?

MAX: Thank you.

DIANA: But at least let me leave up the other one.

MAX: You mean the one of Mr. Borden sprawled out on the sofa? That's actually the goriest one.

> *(Pause.)*

Why are you so eager to launch this business so quickly?? Why not go into things more gradually?

DIANA: We've been here for three months! Why not?

MAX: Is this about trying to keep your mind off . . . your divorce? Or . . . getting your confidence back after your business was wiped out?

DIANA: Huh? I got divorced over a year ago. What are you talking about?

MAX: It just seems hasty. It just seems—

DIANA: Don't start bringing up my time in Tulsa and all that. My past is not relevant here.

MAX: Are you sure?

> *(Pause.)*

DIANA: Look. It's true that I *do* want us to have our own path now, Max. I want the bed and breakfast to be run in *our* direction.

MAX: We agreed on that when we inherited it.

DIANA: And yes, I know: I *did* lose everything when I was in Tulsa. But Max, I was the same way with my business there. Aggressive. Business savvy! I want to succeed here!

> *(Pause. She gradually begins to experience a head ache here.)*

MAX: Well. Just don't forget that there are two of us here.
> *(Pause as he thinks.)*
I need you to understand this. Sometimes I get worried. Worried about those pictures on our site and what people might think. And I . . .

DIANA: You *what?*

MAX: I don't know! I'm just concerned that people will get the wrong idea about us! That we're losing our reputation as a respectable business.
> *(Off the anguish on her face.)*
You okay?

DIANA: Yes, I'm fine. Max, what other ideas would people have? I mean, we're not a wedding chapel or a place to have birthday parties!
> *(Pause. More pain from the headache.)*
I'll take down the picture, Max. We can compromise, can't we?

MAX: Yes. We can. But is there anything else you're working on that you want to let me in on?

DIANA: Well, no. Not really.

MAX: Not *really*? No *searching for prussic acid?*

DIANA: No!

MAX: What about that television commercial? What's that going to cost?

DIANA: It'll be cheap! I'll give you the details when I find out everything. I've forgotten the actual price. But it could really bring business, Max. Loads of it!

MAX: Whatever. What *is* the Chill Channel, anyway? Horror movies?

DIANA: Uh, yeah. Basically.

(He sighs, picks up a clipboard and turns to exit.)

MAX: All right, sis, let's communicate. Don't do anything else crazy without talking to me first. Let's don't screw up what we have here. I don't want to go back to working for the post office.

DIANA: Max?

MAX: What?

DIANA: You ever . . . do you ever have bad dreams?

MAX: Bad dreams? Nightmares? No.

DIANA: Oh.

MAX: Why?

DIANA: Just wondering. You know, I think about them sometimes.

MAX: It's those horror movies you watch.

DIANA: No, I haven't watched any of those lately. Seriously.

MAX: Well . . . I don't know. This place isn't messing with you, is it?

DIANA: No, of course not. Please.
     (Forces a fake laugh.)
I just have these crazy dreams sometimes.

MAX: Alright. Well. You gonna be okay?

DIANA: Yes. I'll be fine. Just need more rest.

MAX: Alright. I've got to go to the bank. Take your aspirin.

     (Exits. The same single light and deep note of music accompany this mini-scene. Diana walks over to the wall, pulls out notepad and tape measure, checks

one measurement on the wall, writes it down. She continues to experience the headache, then gradually resumes with the measurements.)

*(**LIZZIE** walks out, as before, and silently observes Diana. She remains there until the light fades. End of scene.)*

SCENE THREE

A few days later. As the lights go up, DIANA is wiping the countertops/tables with a wet rag, working, speaking to JACK by speaker-phone.

DIANA: Yeah. I understand. Look, I just want to be sure that I won't be facing anything legal if I go through with this.

JACK: Well, that's what I was telling you. When Stanford Law School did a mock trial of the Lizzie Borden case in 1997, some people were concerned that was what might happen.

DIANA: So . . . what happened?

JACK: Well, it was just a mock trial at a university so basically *nothing* happened. And I don't think that it affected the bed and breakfast. But some members of the Borden family did issue a statement, claiming they weren't comfortable with it.

DIANA: Really?

JACK: Yes. Now . . . that was sixteen years ago. But think about it: what if you really *did* uncover an old bottle of prussic acid inside that wall? Is that what it's called? Prussic acid?

DIANA: Yes.

JACK: Okay, well, imagine if that really *is* in there. She supposedly tried to poison them with that, right?

DIANA: Yes.

JACK: Be careful of what you ask for. No matter what the speculation is, you know that the Bordens were killed by an axe, not by poison. What you're doing could ruffle some feathers somewhere. Your parents were the owners there for a long time. But remember, they weren't part of the Borden family. Neither are you. Rest assured, there are distant members of the Borden family out there somewhere.

DIANA: Yeah.

JACK: And also, Diana, you've got to remind yourself: Lizzie Borden was never found guilty. An excavation like that could be disastrous.

> *(Pause. Enter MAX, wearing rubber gloves and carrying a bucket.)*

DIANA: Or it could be successful.

JACK: Well, yeah, that too.

DIANA: I appreciate it, Jack. I always know who to call when it comes to this kind of stuff.

JACK: That it?

DIANA: *(Hurriedly, due to MAX.)* Yes. That's it. Gotta go.

JACK: Anytime, Diana. Take care. I'm glad you're back in New England.

DIANA: Thanks. Bye.

(Hangs up. Pause.)

MAX: Who was that?

DIANA: Oh, nobody. Old college friend. He's a lawyer. I had to ask him something about my divorce. What are you doing?

MAX: It's those people in rooms seven and eight. You know, the goth group.

DIANA: Oh yeah. Interesting bunch.

MAX: 'Interesting' is putting it mildly. I just cleaned candle wax off the nightstands in both of their rooms.

DIANA: Candle wax?

MAX: They had candles all over the place in there. Looks like some kind of seance was going on.

(Pause.)

You know them, right?

DIANA: Well, they're some friends of Keith. You remember Keith.

MAX: Yes. But, damn. They were here for three days. Did they use that weekday discount thing we ran a while back?

DIANA: Yes.

MAX: Figures.

> *(He goes to computer, works. DIANA's headache gradually begins again, and it escalates throughout the scene.)*

DIANA: Well, sorry. What do you want me to say? They're customers that took advantage of a travel coupon. I didn't ask them to light candles in the room.

MAX: They were also up all night last night. I heard them. I don't know how we didn't get any complaints.

DIANA: Well . . .

(Pause. The telephone rings, and she picks up.)

Borden House, can I help you?

(Pause.)

Oh, yes. Yeah, I'm sorry. We are booked Halloween night.

(Pause.)
Yes, that's right! Sorry.
        (Pause.)
Okay. Thank you. Bye!
        (Hangs up.)

MAX: Diana . . . those pictures are still on the site.

DIANA: Oh. God. I totally forgot, Max.

MAX: You said you'd—

DIANA: I know, I know. I'll take care of it. I haven't been feeling very well.

MAX: Today?

DIANA: Huh?

MAX: Can you do it today?

DIANA: Max, we already have so much to do today.

MAX: I'd feel a lot better if they were off the website as soon as possible. I . . . *(Beat. Reading the screen.)* What's this email?
        (Pause as he reads.)
A reporter from the Eagle? What . . . ?

DIANA: Shit. He used the hotel email?

MAX: Yes.

DIANA: Sorry. He's supposed to email *me*. It's just a writer.

MAX: Huh?

DIANA: He wants to do a feature on us as the new owners.

MAX: Are you sure that's all he's interested in?

DIANA: Well, I don't think he's interested in *me*.

MAX: Don't be cute. That's not what I mean. He says here that 'he has a particular interest in the potential tear-down of the wall.' I'm looking right at it.

> *(Pause. She puts her hands to her head, in great pain here.)*

MAX: Those pictures on the web are one thing. And I'm not going to even bring up that ridiculous TV commercial. But—

DIANA: You just did.

MAX: What's going on around here, Diana? Everything is just—just—

DIANA: Just WHAT?

MAX: Everything's spiraling in a certain DIRECTION! That's what! Reporters! Séances!

DIANA: How do you know there was a séance in that room??

MAX: Why don't we talk about the wall? That's what I'm really concerned about! You lied to me. What the hell are you trying to pull?

DIANA: I'm not trying to pull anything!

MAX: We agreed that we weren't going to do a tear-down! You told me you were going to drop that whole prussic acid thing!

DIANA: It's just an email.

MAX: But you promised me that you weren't going to pursue that! And now a local newspaper knows about it??

DIANA: Why are you flipping out all of a sudden?

MAX: Because we are losing any sense of Mom and Dad's honorable ways! That's why!

DIANA: Please!

MAX: I know, Diana. About Tulsa.

(Pause. Heavy beat.)

DIANA: What?

MAX: I know about Tulsa. I know that you filed bankruptcy long before that tornado wiped your business out. I know.

(Pause.)

DIANA: Who told you?

MAX: I talked to Kevin. He called and . . . we started talking. It all came out.

DIANA: He called?

MAX: He called.

DIANA: What the hell did he want?

MAX: He needed some information, something about some tax papers from when you guys were married. It sounded important.

DIANA: Shit. He already has all that stuff.

MAX: I told him to email you. The point is he called, and we started talking. And it all came out.
(Pause.)
And I think I'm beginning to connect the dots here.

DIANA: Whatever. What happened in Oklahoma has nothing to do with all of this.

MAX: Well, whatever it was, I don't even care. We're family. We'll move forward.

DIANA: Are you sure?

MAX: Yes, I'm sure! But I see the way you've been acting since you got back. And I'm really concerned that whatever happened out there is affecting you here!

DIANA: You can stop worrying because it's not!

MAX: But that's *exactly* what's happening! I know you. You're an overachiever. Your ambition . . . and pride. How this whole thing with the wall can bring the business more recognition, fame, and—

DIANA: I never said I *absolutely* wanted to go through with the excavation! All I did was contact that reporter!

MAX: Would it make you happier if we just went ahead and did it ourselves?

DIANA: What are you talking about?

MAX: Here! The tool box is right down here!
(He furiously grabs it from under desk.)
Let's just get it out of the way. Forget about decency! About respect! Let's just make this place the lobby to hell!

DIANA: *(In enormous pain.)* No.

MAX: Come on! Why not? Your persistence has no end. You said so yourself!

DIANA: NO!!

MAX: I'm worn out by all of this, Diana!! Seriously!! Let's just DO IT!!

DIANA: I said NO!!

> *(She grabs the toolbox and slings it to the floor with a crash. Long pause. They catch their breath.)*

MAX: Sorry. I . . . I shouldn't have.

> *(Pause. DIANA walks off, paces.)*

DIANA: I . . . found some of Mom's old diaries and letters, Max. They were in that box from the attic.

> *(Pause.)*

MAX: And . . . ?

DIANA: It's in there. In Mom's diaries. In her writing. You were right. I can't believe I'm actually admitting to this . . . but she would *never* want us to do this wall teardown. *They* would never want it. I've been trying to tell myself otherwise. But you were right.

(Pause.)
And I'm not so sure that *other* people would want us to do it either.

MAX: What are you saying?

DIANA: I'm asking you . . . if you can forgive me for being so bullheaded around here. So . . *hasty*, as you would say.

MAX: Well . . .

DIANA: I'll take those pictures down from the site. I'll drop the whole idea. The tear-down. Emailing that reporter. Everything. And I'll try to chill out.
(Pause. Closes eyes, puts hands to temples.)
I think that my headaches . . . well, let's just say that the house may have something to do with them.

(Telephone rings)

MAX: I'll get that.

DIANA: No, let me. I'm fine. I got it.
(Picks up.)
Borden House?
(Pause.)
Excuse me? Oh. Okay. Yes. Yes, ten o'clock. Right, it's on our calendar. We're all set. Thank you.
(Hangs up. Pause.)

That was the termite guy. He'll be here Halloween morning. Ha—of all days.

MAX: Diana . . . are you okay?

DIANA: Yeah. I think I am. I really do.

MAX: Are you sure? I'm almost scared to ask . . .

DIANA: So don't then. Seriously, it's fine. I'm okay.
(Pause. Takes a breath.)
Max, you are right. Our business is doing well. But I'm just . . . over-anxious sometimes. I *do* let ambition get the best of me. I have to admit: Tulsa really did a number on me. You have no idea. And I believe maybe something *here* has done a number on me as well. But I think it'll be fine.
(Pause as she reflects.)
One day we'll talk about it. But for now, this wall needs to stay the way that it is.

MAX: Do you really think there's a bottle of prussic acid somewhere in that wall?

DIANA: A lot of people certainly think so. The so-called Lizzie Borden scholars. But as for me . . . I don't think I want to know.
(Pause. She rubs her head.)
I don't think I *ever* want to know.

(He goes to pick up the tools.)

DIANA: No, I'll take care of that. Can you . . . give me a minute here alone, Max?

MAX: Yeah. I guess so.

DIANA: Can you get those towels for room nine? Please?

MAX*:* You're sure you're okay?

DIANA: I'm fine. *(Pause.)* I'm fine.

MAX: *(Begins to exit.)* Okay.

DIANA: Hey . . .

MAX: Yeah?

DIANA: Mom and Dad's honorable ways, huh?

> *(Pause.)*

MAX: That's right. Mom and Dad's honorable ways. Even in the Lizzie Borden house.

> *(He exits. She pauses for a moment, putting her fingertips to her forehead, relaxing. She walks to the wall, touches it with one hand, deep in thought.*
>
> *(LIZZIE enters far stage left or right, one final time, and observes. When DIANA turns and slowly*

walks over to pick up the tools, LIZZIE exits. Lights fade. End of play.)

✍ **Alternate ending** ✍

This is an option for the very end of the play. It simply replaces the stage directions above that begin with "He exits."

He exits. DIANA pauses for a moment, putting her fingertips to her forehead, relaxing. She walks to the wall, touches it with one hand, deep in thought.

Suddenly, DIANA swiftly turns and marches to the tool box, picks up a large hammer or hatchet. Long pause as DIANA holds the tool and focuses on it. LIZZIE enters far stage left or right, one final time, and observes. DIANA slowly turns and walks toward the wall, still holding the tool. LIZZIE begins to walk toward DIANA, without her knowing it. The lights slowly fade. The long note is heard as the lights fade. End of play.

Hockey Masks in Hueytown

-

A one-act play

by
John Glass

☞   ☞

Hockey Masks in Hueytown

<u>Characters</u>

TAMAREH   College student. Snippy.
                  Impatient. Attitude.

JEREMY   College student. Somewhat
                  relaxed.

JASMINE   College student. Patient.
                  Easygoing.

DAN   College student. Slacker.
                  Laid back.

The setting is the present. It is late Wednesday afternoon of Thanksgiving week. The scene is an attic of a
house in a small town. The lighting is somewhat dim.
There are stacks of boxes everywhere, the scene of a
typical attic.

The lighting to this play is critical. Starting on page 71, after Jeremy pulls the mask off, the lights gradually become even dimmer. This should be extremely gradual and very subtle. The "wall" at the end of the play could be anything solid or wooden, right behind a curtain stage left or right. Any prop or piece of furniture would work, a bureau, etc.

The play could easily be altered to fit a high school cast. In that event, the characters would be attending a boarding school and are all driving home for Thanksgiving break.

Setting: the attic of an old house. The stage is completely dark. One light goes up, not too bright. The four students slowly enter the attic.

JEREMY: Well. This is it.

TAMAREH: Is that the only light up here?

JEREMY: Yeah, I think so. There's only one light switch here so . . .

JASMINE: Wow.

DAN: Damn. Kind of scary.

JEREMY: So, here we are.

JASMINE: This is it? The collection of your late uncle?

JEREMY: I guess so. Mr. Hollywood himself.

TAMAREH: *(Snidely)* Well, whatever you guys do, don't tell my boyfriend I was crawling around the attic of a house in the middle of *Hueytown.*

JASMINE: This is cool!

JEREMY: Man . . . I don't think anybody's been in here for years.

DAN: It shows. Look at all this dust!

JASMINE: Well . . . Jeremy, can we, you know, go ahead and dive in?

JEREMY: Of course. That's why we're here. Look for them. Red and black picture albums.

JASMINE: Let's do it.

DAN: *(Sitting down.)* You guys knock yourselves out.

JEREMY: There's actually a lot more junk in there than I thought.

TAMAREH: Didn't you have *any* idea it was like this?

JEREMY: I told you, this is my first time in here. I knew my aunt saved a lot of his stuff after he died. But I didn't know she had this much.
    (Beat. He opens a box.)
Look at all these books.

DAN: No thank you. Books are the *last* thing I want to see right now. I've had my face stuck in Shakespeare for the last two weeks.

TAMAREH: Yeah, I'm sure your final exam won't reflect that.

DAN: Smart ass.

JASMINE: Wow. Magazines all over the place. *(Reading the titles.)* Creepy. Fangoria. Spinefest??

DAN: He really was into the Halloween stuff, wasn't he?

TAMAREH: Um, duhh. He worked on Friday the 13th, genius.

DAN: Oh, that's right. *(Sarcastically)* Big-time Hollywood guy!

JEREMY: No, just a part-time production guy. Part-time carpenter. Nothing more.

TAMAREH: Let's just get this out of the way so we can get back on the road. What are the pictures in? Photo albums?

JEREMY: Old photo albums. Red and black.

JASMINE: *(Going through a new box.)* Tape measures. A case of drill bits. Whaa . .? Why are there jars of coffee in here??

DAN: Now, *that's* creepy. *(Pulling out cigarettes)* Mind if I smoke in here?

JEREMY: Uhh—

TAMAREH: Dude, put that away!

DAN: Why?

TAMAREH: It's an attic, imbecile! It's already cramped in here as it is!

JASMINE: Yeah, Dan. Please don't smoke.

DAN: *(Getting up to exit.)* Okay, whatever. I'm going downstairs. I'm going to be the first person to show any common sense here.

TAMAREH: Huh?

DAN: Uh, hello . . ?? We're college kids, stopped off in a strange town to go inside someone's *attic*? This is how stupid things happen!

JEREMY: Whatever, man. It's my aunt's house.

DAN: I'll be downstairs. I'm gonna go out to that back patio and smoke a cigarette.

JEREMY: Well, stay in that area. We don't need the neighbors wondering what a bunch of strangers are doing here.

JASMINE: Your aunt knows that we're here, right?

JEREMY: Yes. But it's better if we're not walking around on her property.

DAN: Okay. You guys hurry up.

JEREMY: Don't touch anything.

DAN: I won't, Dad.
(*Exits.*)

TAMAREH: That boy can't go fifteen minutes without his Marlboro Lights.

JASMINE: Check these out . . . more Creepy magazines.

JEREMY: Cool.

JASMINE: A tool belt. And, ha! Look! A mannequin hand! *(Pulling it from the box.)*

JEREMY: Whoa!

JASMINE: I love this!

TAMAREH: I don't know why you aren't majoring in Halloween Studies.

JEREMY: Geez. My aunt was right. Apparently, my uncle *did* have a screw loose.

TAMAREH: Uh, you think?? *Creepy* magazines? A jar of coffee? The hand of a mannequin? I don't see any pictures, though.

JEREMY: Well, they're here.

TAMAREH: You don't plan on going through all this stuff, do you?

JEREMY: Well . . . no. Not necessarily.

JASMINE: Tamareh, you knew what we came in here for!

TAMAREH: Well, sort of. But what I remember *most* are Jeremy's words while we were in the car:
(*Quoting him.*)
"I just want to stop and quickly check out something in my aunt's attic."
(*Pause as she repeats, using air quotes*)
"Quickly check." I mean, this sucks. There's a ton of stuff in here to look through! Plus, we had to drive thirty miles off the freeway, which means we have to drive thirty miles back. I'd like to get home and enjoy my weekend.

JEREMY: Would you chill out? It's a four day weekend. What's your rush??

TAMAREH: Hmmpphh.

JEREMY: We're only about three hours from Baltimore. We'll be outta here in no time.

JASMINE: Jeremy? Have you considered . . . that those pictures may *not* be here?

JEREMY: No. They're here. I'm convinced of that. My aunt's told my mother many times that they were in this attic somewhere. They're very old pictures. And I'd really love for my mom to be able to have them.

JASMINE: What time is your aunt coming home to-day?

JEREMY: Uh, around six. After she gets off work.

JASMINE: Six?

JEREMY: Yep.

(*TAMAREH pulls out an old Halloween vampire mask.*)

TAMAREH: Now . . . this is actually pretty sweet.

JEREMY: Ugghh!

JASMINE: Wow. That thing is old!

JEREMY: *Everything* in here is old. Take it if you want it.

TAMAREH: Why the hell would I want this?? I have no use for it.

JASMINE: Tamareh, you could wear it at Chad's house tomorrow while eating Thanksgiving dinner! You could really freak that family out.

TAMAREH: Please.
(*Tossing the mask aside.*)
His parents are so square they'd have a heart attack.

JASMINE: (*Snatching the mask, looking it over*)

Give me that.

TAMAREH: Ha, if I ever *get* to Chad's house.
    (Beat. To JEREMY)
So . . . you're one-hundred percent certain that those pictures are in here? Sure that your aunt didn't get rid of them?

JEREMY: I'm sure. I hardly know my aunt but I do know that this attic freaks her out.

TAMAREH: Um. Why?

JEREMY: I don't know. She told my mother that she never comes up here by herself. So . . .

JASMINE: That's strange.

JEREMY: Yeah. She . . . she said that this attic was part of why she and my uncle divorced.

TAMAREH: Excuse me?

JEREMY: Yeah, I know. It's dumb.

JASMINE: Weird.

JEREMY: That's my aunt: weird.

TAMAREH: How could a *room* of someone's house contribute to their divorce?

JEREMY: No idea. My aunt is loopy. Kind of an odd-ball.

JASMINE: Like, worse than your uncle?

JEREMY: Don't know. I only know that this attic is a touchy subject for her. I told you guys, my family isn't that close. I haven't talked to my aunt in over a year.

> *(Pause. TAMAREH and JASMINE stop working and look at him.)*

TAMAREH: Wait. What??

JEREMY: Yeah . . . I haven't. It's been a while . . . *(His voice trails off.)*

JASMINE: I thought she knew we were here??

JEREMY: *(Weakly.)* She does.

TAMAREH: But you haven't talked to her in over a year?? What's going on, Jeremy? How does she know we're in her house if you guys haven't spoken in over a year?

> *(Pause. JEREMY is flattened with guilt)*

JEREMY: Okay, I lied. Sorry.

TAMAREH: What the hell . . ? We're gonna get arrested for breaking and entering?? On Thanksgiving weekend??

JEREMY: Would you shut up? We're not going to get arrested!

TAMAREH: You lied to us! What are we *really* doing here??

JEREMY: We are looking for old pictures of my family! How many times do you need me to repeat that??

TAMAREH: Then why did you lie about your aunt?

JASMINE: Jeremy, she's not going to suddenly come home, is she? I don't want any trouble.

JEREMY: Look. I'm sorry. I shouldn't have lied to you guys. My aunt isn't even in the country. She's in Portugal for three months, visiting some people.

JASMINE: What??

JEREMY: I just didn't want you guys to think we were, you know, *sneaking* in here.

TAMAREH: But that's exactly what we're doing! Right?

JEREMY: No. My aunt told my mother years ago that she wouldn't care if we came and took everything out of here. You know, if we were ever in Hueytown. Seriously, this attic really *does* freak her out. And according to my mom, my aunt spends very little time in this house. She wouldn't mind at all that we're here.

(Pause as they take all of this in.)

TAMAREH: So how did you get the spare key to this house? I thought your families weren't that close!

JEREMY: I've had it. I took it from our junk drawer in the kitchen. When I was home this summer. That spare key's been in there for years.
(Pause.)
No big deal.

TAMAREH: No big deal . .?

JEREMY: That's right. Honestly. My aunt really is in Portugal. This house has been empty for weeks.

(Pause.)

JASMINE: Well. Shoot. Jeremy, if you're comfortable being here, then I guess I'm comfortable being here. *(She slowly resumes her search)*

JEREMY: Everything's cool. Okay? We'll just find these pictures and then we'll get out of here. Nothing to worry about.

TAMAREH: If you say so.

JEREMY: I'm sorry I lied. Honestly, I'm ready to leave myself.

TAMAREH: Something told me catching a ride with you was a mistake.

JEREMY: And something told *me* that letting you in my car was an even bigger mistake!

JASMINE: Easy, you guys.

TAMAREH: *(To JEREMY)* Excuse me??

JEREMY: You've been bitching for the whole ride.
(Mimics her, in a sarcastic whine.)
"I need to go to the bathroom. Can we stop and get a Coke? Can you go any faster??"

TAMAREH: Whatever. This is stupid.

JASMINE: *(Pulling out a hockey mask from a box)* Uh . . . guys?

TAMAREH: The only reason I came into this house was because you're driving us to Baltimore and I felt obligated. But what a joke. I would take a bus home right now. If there *were* any in this podunk-ass town.

JEREMY: *(Staring at the mask.)* Wow. You found it!

JASMINE: Check it out.

TAMAREH: It's a Jason mask. Big deal.

JEREMY: Jasmine, you *found* it!

JASMINE: There are actually two masks here.

JEREMY: Yep!

TAMAREH: What's the big deal? You knew those things were in here?

JASMINE: They're, like, solid, and heavy.

JEREMY: Nice!!

JASMINE: *(Examining it closely)* And look right here . . . what does that say? *(Reading.)* "Prop 9. Friday the 13th, Part 3. Paramount Pictures. July 1983."

JEREMY: Sweet. Good job, Jas!

JASMINE: So . . these are the real deal? From the actual "Friday the 13th"?

JEREMY: Yep. I think so. *(He raises the mask to his face.)* What do you think?

JASMINE: Yeahh! Okay, I have to get a picture of this! Hang on, my camera's in my backpack.

TAMAREH: Jasmine, wait! Just do it when we leave!

JASMINE: No, I want a picture while we're in the attic.

TAMAREH: I'm ready to get out of here! Hurry!

JASMINE: *(Exiting)* I will! Come on, how many times in your life are you going to see a hockey mask in an attic? In a place called *Hueytown*??

TAMAREH: Never again, I hope.

JASMINE: Be right back!

> *(JASMINE exits. TAMAREH starts digging into a box as JEREMY puts the mask on.)*

TAMAREH: Well. Screw this. I'm gonna look in this one box and if I don't see any pictures I'm headed downstairs. I'm ready to get back on the road.
> *(Looks at him. He is wearing the mask and looking at her.)*
Would you take that thing off??

JEREMY: Why? It's cool.

TAMAREH: Yeah, if you're into weirdos that walk around with steak knives and try to kill people.

JEREMY: I like it.

TAMAREH: Ughh. Come on. Keep looking.

> *(He pulls it off slowly, then gathers the other mask. From this point forward, the light should gradually become dimmer. This goes on until they put the masks back on.)*

JEREMY: Well. Actually, I guess I'm ready to go too.

TAMAREH: Huh?

JEREMY: Yeah. We can probably go downstairs now.

TAMAREH: We're leaving?

JEREMY: Yeah. Jas can just take a picture of the mask outside.

TAMAREH: Don't you want those pictures??

JEREMY: Of course. But they're probably not here.

TAMAREH: We've hardly looked! All you've talked about was finding your mother's childhood pictures. And now . . ?

JEREMY: Well, we *did* look. I'm just beginning to think they're not here.

TAMAREH: This is stupid! Why did we even come up here?
> *(She slams the box back down on table. Beat. She looks at him.)*
Wait . . . wait a second. Why are we *really* here?? Did we come into this house to look for those masks??

JEREMY: No!

TAMAREH: Is that why we're here, Jeremy? Are you looking for a fast buck?

JEREMY: No!

TAMAREH: I can't believe this . . *(Voice trails off)*

JEREMY: That's *not* why we're here.

TAMAREH: Ughh!!

JEREMY: *(Looking up at the light.).* Hey. Um. I . . . I think something is up with the light in here.

TAMAREH: I should have never gotten into your car!

JEREMY: Listen, we should probably leave! I think the light is about to go out! *(Begins to exit.)*

TAMAREH: Fine by me. This whole thing has been a complete joke.

JEREMY: Come on!

> *(She throws a few of the scattered items back into the box and begins to exit. JEREMY is already at the door, where he comes to an abrupt stop.)*

JEREMY: Okay . . what is this? *(He bangs on the door/wall)* Tamareh . . ?

TAMAREH: *(Joining him.)* What is it?

JEREMY: There's a wall here, that's what!

TAMAREH: What the . . ?

JEREMY: Right where the doorway was!

TAMAREH: I don't believe this.

JEREMY: *(Bangs on the wall again.)* DAN!! JAS-MINE!!

TAMAREH: This is *not* happening.

JEREMY: Why is there suddenly a wall here? There's no doorknob. There's no door. Just a . .
> *(He bangs on it again, with furious desperation.)*
JASMINE!!

TAMAREH: It's like it was always here.

JEREMY: Tamareh, what do we do?? It's getting even darker in here.

(Pause as they stare at each other.)

TAMAREH: Look . . ever since you pulled off that hockey mask it's been dimmer and dimmer in here.

JEREMY: What??

TAMAREH: It's true, Jeremy. I noticed it right away. But I just thought I was imagining things.

JEREMY: *(Staring at the mask, dumbfounded.)* Is this . . ?

TAMAREH: Something's going on. Maybe your aunt *was* right about this attic.

JEREMY: It's even darker!

TAMAREH: *(Grabbing the other mask, putting it on.)*
Put the mask on!

JEREMY: Why??

TAMAREH: Just do it!! I can't explain any of this!! But I told you, the second you pulled it off, the light began to fade. Do it, Jeremy!!

> *(Both of them put the masks on. Pause. They breathe heavily and look at each other.)*

JEREMY: Is it working?

TAMAREH: I don't know. I think so.

> *(Pause. They collect themselves.)*

JEREMY: *(Sobbing)* Oh, Tamareh . . I'm sorry. I am so sorry. What you said was true. I *did* bring you guys up here to look for these masks.

TAMAREH: You knew they were in here all along.

JEREMY: They're worth a lot of money. A *lot* of money.
> *(Pause.)*
And I was too scared to come in here by myself. Even though I had no idea this attic was like this. . .
> *(Pause. His sobbing increases.)*
But . . what the hell . . ? It's almost like . . this mask *activated* something. That wall . . the light . .

TAMAREH: *(Looking at her phone)* My phone is completely dead.

JEREMY: Ohh! And mine's in the car!! What do we do??

TAMAREH: We're going to find a way out of here! *That's* what!

JEREMY: How??

TAMAREH: Get a hold of yourself! Let's help each other out here!

> *(Pause as he continues to lightly sob and stare at her.)*

TAMEREH: Okay? Now, look. Your uncle worked as a carpenter, right?

JEREMY: Yes.

TAMAREH: Well, come on, then. There may be other tools in these boxes.

JEREMY: What's that going to do??

TAMAREH: Look at how old these floorboards are!! If we find a hammer or something maybe we can break through!
> *(JEREMY pauses, and just stares at her.)*
Right??

*(She begins to rifle through the boxes but
JEREMY is still standing, in a daze. She stops
and grabs his arms.)*

TAMAREH: Jeremy!! DON'T YOU GIVE UP ON ME!!

JEREMY: Where are Dan and Jasmine?? Why didn't
they answer us??

TAMAREH: I don't know! Believe me, I'm just as ter-
rified as you are! I don't know what the hell is happening. But we can either stand here and bitch or we can
do something!!

JEREMY: I know . .

TAMAREH: Come on, we've got to start *somewhere*!
Two masks—ha—are better than one.
        (Pause.)
Right?

JEREMY: Right. *(He slowly joins her in looking
through the boxes.)* Man . . . Tamareh, thanks for being so strong.

TAMAREH: Well. I know I can sometimes be a huge
pain in the ass.

JEREMY: That's not as bad as being a *liar.*

TAMAREH: Just promise me one thing.

JEREMY: What?

TAMAREH: *(Attempting some humor)* After we get out of here, ha, promise me you won't tell anybody that I was crawling around an attic. In the middle of a place called *Hueytown. (Pause as they pant heavily, while working. She stops working and touches his arm.)* Deal?

(Pause. He looks at her.)

JEREMY: Deal.

TAMAREH: We'll find something to help us get out of here. Everything's going to be fine.

(Pause as they continue to dig through the boxes, slowly calming down. The stage suddenly goes completely black.)

TAMAREH: Ohh! What the . . ?

JEREMY: Oh no.

TAMAREH: Jeremy?
(Pause.)
JEREMY?!?

(Pause. She screams loudly, one time. A long note of music is heard, just like at the play's beginning. Silence. End of play.)

☞ More from Student Plays ☜

Othello's Just Another Fellow

Dramedy. **Grades 5-7.** 25-35 minutes. 8 actors: 4 males, 3 females, one teacher (or student portraying a teacher) 3 to 5 extras, if needed. ****A Latino-themed play****

A group of students are involved in a school production of *Othello*, but one of them is disturbed about the lack of diversity in the play. He takes certain steps to disrupt the play but in the end is encouraged by the others to try and make a difference in another, more constructive way. A lesson is learned, and the production is saved from disaster!

Pagasqueeny's Pantry

Comedy. **Middle/High School.** 15-20 minutes. 6 actors: 3 females, 2 males. One student (or a teacher) plays the comical role of the elderly Mr. Pagasqueeny.

Three friends sneak into Mr. Pagasqueeny's home to get something that one of them left behind. But in walks Pagasqueeny and they must hide in the pantry! In this comical play, a lesson is learned about honesty and trust, but it takes a heated discussion in the pantry and a subsequent attempt to escape to find this out!

Una Carta de Abuelo

Dramedy. **Middle/High School.** 35-45 minutes. 10 actors: 1 teacher, 5 females, 4 males. (With the option of 4-5 extra actors in two scenes.)   ****A Latino-themed play****

Two cousins discover an old letter in their late grandfather's comic collection that they think leads to treasure! The cousins often butt heads, with one believing that he is more "Mexican," the other believing that some people make too much of a fuss about "being Mexican." Thus, they form their *own* groups in search of what Grandpa hid long ago. But what they find is actually worth more than merely silver or gold.

Barbecue at the Prom!

Dramedy. **Grades 5-8.** 25-35 minutes. 6 actors: 3 females, 3 males

It's a classic tale of guys versus girls! It's a prom committee, and everybody is supposed to work together but differences and opinions get in the way, causing the guys and girls to form their groups. For the end-of-the-year prom, one side wants pasta and lace, the other wants sports and barbecue! The two groups square off but eventually work together, demonstrating the importance of cooperation and compromise.

Going to Guatemala

Dramedy. **High School.** 50-60 minutes. 11 actors. 6 males, 5 females.   ****A Latino-themed play****

A Latino student is chosen at the last minute to join a humanitarian group from his school that is headed to Guatemala. But since his Spanish is weak, he faces ridicule and criticism from certain peers. Jealousy and anger trickle throughout the campus as the trip approaches, and the social buzz of the high school becomes even more hectic when the student's trip money is stolen on campus, jeopardizing his trip.

Stravinsky's Kitchen

Comedy. **High School/College.** 12-15 minutes. 3 actors: 3 males (or females).

Two friends secretly enter the home of an employer to obtain a forgotten object but the homeowner abruptly arrives home while they are there. As they hide in the kitchen's pantry and plot their getaway, the two talk and eventually argue, exposing the true colors of one of them. Upon their hasty exit a mistake is made, and one of them capitalizes on this mistake, resulting in his/her fortune.

Forty Whacks

Drama. Spooky. **High School/College.** 25-35 minutes. 3 actors: 2 females, 1 male.

A pair of siblings have inherited the Lizzie Borden Bed and Breakfast in New England. Although the business was run for decades in a quiet, respectable fashion, one of the siblings is over-ambitious, wanting to unearth an alleged piece of buried evidence within the house. This brings about a chilly tension between brother and sister, and perhaps within the house itself.

John Calhoun and a Thief

Drama. **College.** 35-40 minutes. 3 actors: 2 females, 1 male.

Kicked out of a university PhD program, a bitter and dejected female lifts from the library archives original copies of John Calhoun's personal documents. Counseled and consoled by her roommates, her conscience slowly gets to her; but as she seeks entry to other universities her luck turns to worse, and the subsequent decisions she makes regarding the historic papers cause this one-act play to become darker, if not funnier.

Honoring the Hijacker

Drama. **College.** 12-15 minutes. 4 actors: 2 females, 2 males.

It's 1981, the ten-year anniversary of the famed hijacker D.B. Cooper. The play's four characters are attending a "D.B. Festival" and have stayed up very late, outlasting everybody else. The late night chit-chat goes from pranks and jokes to outright volatility, and suddenly this get-together becomes something that three of the four characters didn't bargain for.

It's a Super Day at Sammy's!

Comedy. **Middle or High School.** 35-40 minutes. 9 actors: 5 females, 4 males (4 possible adults).

Jodi has found a summer job at a travel agency. But her three younger siblings can't seem to live without her! They call her at the office incessantly, which interferes with the work. The standard telephone greeting "It's a super day at Sammy's!" becomes a repeated theme of this comedy, as Jodi struggles to reach a balance between her job and her nagging siblings

Three Tenners

Comedy/Drama. **Elementary through High School.** Three Ten-Minute Plays.

Three Creepy Plays

Drama. **Middle School through College.** Three short 'creepy' plays.

Hockey Masks in Hueytown

Drama. Spooky. **High School/College.** 20-25 minutes. 4 actors: 2 males, 2 females.

Driving home for Thanksgiving break, four college students stop off in a small rural town to retrieve one of the student's old family pictures. They reluctantly enter the empty home of his deceased uncle, a former producer for the Friday the 13th movies. Strange objects are found during their search . . but when a hockey mask surfaces, everything really goes sideways.

The Witch Makes Five

Drama. Spooky. **High School.** 10 minutes. 4 actors: 2 males, 2 females.

After a bizarre group camping trip, a student is checked into a youth mental facility . When she is visited by the other members of the trip, memories of the weekend trickle out . . . and horrific things begin to happen.

Mrs. Calapooza and the Culebra

Dramedy. **Grades 5-8.** 10 minutes. 5 actors: 3 females, 2 males.

Fed up with their grouchy teacher's classroom ways, four students complain and bicker back and forth during a Spanish quiz. The situation grows worse when the friends discover that one of them has pulled the ultimate prank on the teacher.

Raiders of the Lost Rakasa

Dramedy. **Grades 5-8.** 10 minutes. 7 actors: 4 females, 3 males.

Seven young explorers arrive at a cave in a far-off land in search of the great "Rakasa." They find what they want . . . along with a few of the cave's unexpected surprises.